Hurricane!

NATURE'S DISASTERS

Hurricane!

Jules Archer

A LUCAS · EVANS BOOK

CRESTWOOD HOUSE
New York
Collier Macmillan Canada
Toronto
Maxwell Macmillan International Publishing Group
New York   Oxford   Singapore   Sydney

For Sunny and her grandchildren:
Robert, Juanita, Justin, Lacey and Nicole

COVER: Radar image of Hurricane Hugo off the coast of Florida.
FRONTIS: Hurricane damage at Biloxi, Mississippi.
PAGE 7: Satellite picture of a hurricane, sharply depicting the eye of the storm.

PHOTO CREDITS: *Cover,* Susan Greenwood, National Hurricane Center, NOAA; *Frontis,* Air Weather Service/Public Affairs; *Page 7,* Air Weather Service/Public Affairs; *Pages 8–9,* National Hurricane Center, NOAA; *Page 11,* Susan Greenwood, National Hurricane Center, NOAA; *Page 12,* National Hurricane Center, NOAA; *Page 19,* National Hurricane Center, NOAA; *Page 20,* National Hurricane Center, NOAA; *Pages 22, 23,* National Hurricane Center, NOAA; *Page 25,* Air Weather Service/Public Affairs; *Page 26,* Air Weather Service/Public Affairs; *Page 27,* Air Weather Service/Public Affairs; *Pages 28–29,* National Hurricane Center, NOAA; *Page 30,* Air Weather Service/Public Affairs; *Page 31,* National Hurricane Center, NOAA; *Page 32,* Air Weather Service/Public Affairs; *Page 33,* National Hurricane Center, NOAA; *Page 35,* Air Weather Service/Public Affairs; *Page 36,* Air Weather Service/Public Affairs; *Page 38,* National Hurricane Center, NOAA; *Page 41,* National Hurricane Center, NOAA; *Page 42,* Air Weather Service/Public Affairs.

BOOK DESIGN: Barbara DuPree Knowles   DIAGRAMS: Andrew Edwards

LIBRARY OF CONGRESS CATALOGING-IN-PUBLICATION DATA
Archer, Jules.
    Hurricane! / by Jules Archer.—1st ed.
        p.   cm. — (Nature's disasters)
    SUMMARY: Examines the nature, origins, and dangers of hurricanes and discusses the warning system that detects them and alerts people in their path.
    ISBN 0-89686-597-5
    1. Hurricanes—Juvenile literature.   [1. Hurricanes.]   I. Title.   II. Series.
QC944.A73 1991   551.51'.—dc20   90-45369

Crestwood House   Collier Macmillan Canada, Inc.
Macmillan Publishing Company   1200 Eglinton Avenue East
866 Third Avenue   Suite 200
New York, NY 10022   Don Mills, Ontario M3C 3N1
                        First Edition
Printed in the United States of America   10 9 8 7 6 5 4 3 2 1

Contents

Hurricane!

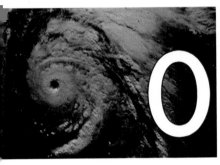

On the tropical island where the author was once stationed, natives called their hurricanes *gubas*. When a guba struck, furious gale winds lashed us with rain torrents blown horizontally. Unless we clung to trees, we were sometimes torn off our feet and rolled along the ground.

One powerful **storm** swept away our tents, Jeeps and equipment. We moved our camp to higher ground. By morning the valley below was flooded under 20 feet of water. Crocodiles and water snakes were swept through the flood currents.

A creek that ran through our new camp quickly became swollen by the drenching rains. Its rapids ripped away a makeshift bridge we used to cross to our mess tent. We fastened a rope between trees, stretching it from one side of the creek to the other. There was danger of being swept away by both the winds and rapids. So we had to hold tight to the rope as we pulled ourselves across the raging waters. It was either that or go hungry.

In 1965 Hurricane Betsy caused Lake Surprise in the Florida Keys to flood and cut off all roads.

Those who have experienced the full force of a powerful hurricane are not likely to forget it for as long as they live. I know I never shall.

GALE WINDS OF DEATH AND DESTRUCTION

In the summer of 1989, storm winds began whirling across the Atlantic from Africa. They sucked up strength from the moist tropical ocean air. Gradually they built into a huge killer storm with 150-mile-an-hour winds. Hurricane Hugo hit Guadeloupe in the Caribbean on September 16. The resort town of St. François was destroyed. Eleven people died.

Next day on Montserrat, Hugo snapped the tops off all the trees and ripped tin roofs off the houses. Doing $100 million worth of damage, the **hurricane** killed ten more people. At St. Kitts, Nevis and St. Croix, it blew 90 percent of the houses into splinters. The north coast of Puerto Rico was left a jumble of smashed towns, toppled trees and twisted power lines. Seven people died, and 90,000 were left homeless. Damage: $300 million.

Hugo then curved north in a fearsome 2,300-mile sweep. **Hurricane warnings** alerted communities along the U.S. coast. The mayor of Charleston, South Carolina, warned that anyone who did not vacate a coastal home in Hugo's path stood a good chance of dying. Over half a million people along the southeast coast fled their homes.

When Hugo reached Charleston, the hurricane carried 20-foot waves. This wall of water smashed into the city's streets. It swept away boats and even a 50-foot yacht. The city hall was flooded and lost its roof. Some 30 major office buildings collapsed. The hurricane left 21 people dead in the Carolinas and Virginia.

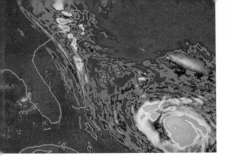

Sept. 20, 9:31 A.M.

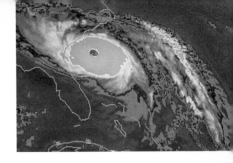

Sept. 21, 11:01 P.M.

Sept. 20, 9:31 P.M.

Sept. 22, 1:01 A.M.

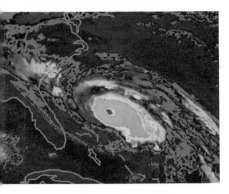

Sept. 21, 10:01 A.M.

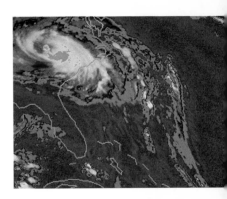

Sept. 22, 11:01 A.M.

Series of radar images of Hurricane Hugo approaching the coast of Florida in September 1989 from the National Hurricane Center, Coral Gables, Florida.

(ABOVE) A handsome house on the South Carolina beach before Hurricane Hugo struck, and (BELOW) what was left of that house after the hurricane passed.

It was considered one of the ten costliest hurricanes ever to hit the U.S. coast. South Carolina alone estimated it had suffered $5 billion in property damage. Before Hugo petered out it took a total of 51 lives.

Wrath of the Ancient Storm Gods

The ancient Greeks believed that a god named Aeolus controlled the winds. He supposedly kept them in a cave that had a dozen holes, blocked by stones. When Aeolus wanted a wind to blow from any direction, he rolled away a stone controlling that wind. To create a hurricane, Aeolus opened all 12 holes.

The Mayas of Central America considered the great storm to be Huracan, a god of big winds and evil spirits. Spanish explorers in the area learned his name from the native people. It became today's word for hurricane. Once a year the Mayan nations sacrificed a young woman to this god to pacify him. She was hurled into the sea. A warrior was sacrificed with her to guide her into the watery kingdom of Huracan.

During Columbus's second voyage to the New World, he built the first European town on the island of Hispaniola. A hurricane promptly wiped it out. In 1500 he sent a fleet of caravels, laden with gold, back to Spain. A hurricane sank 90 ships and drowned 500 sailors. In 1502 Columbus made his final voyage to the New World. In 1503, near what is now Panama, he ran into his first hurricane at sea.

"Eyes never beheld the seas so high, angry and covered by foam," read his awed entry in the ship's log. " . . . We were forced to keep out in this bloody ocean, seething like a pot on a hot fire. Never did the sky look more terrible. . . . All this time the water never ceased to fall from the sky. . . . It was like another deluge. . . . The people were so worn out that they longed for death to end their dreadful suffering."

Hurricanes destroyed hundreds of ships Spain sent to plunder treasure from the New World. As late as the 1980s modern-day treasure hunters were locating some of these ancient wrecks in Florida's waters. They salvaged fortunes in gold and jewels.

A hurricane also shaped part of American history. When the *Mayflower* left England in 1620, it sailed for Virginia, probably for the settlement at Jamestown. But a hurricane blew the ship far off course to the north. The Pilgrims landed in Massachusetts instead.

WHAT IS A HURRICANE?

Where Hurricanes Begin

In the last five centuries, there has never been a year without hurricanes. And each year there has been at least one great hurricane. These large, whirling storms form in the **tropics** over the oceans. When they form in the Atlantic, they are known as hurricanes. When they develop in the Pacific, they are called **typhoons.**

Weather in the tropics—the very warm, humid region north and south of the equator—often goes to extremes. Sometimes there are periods of great calm. Breezes are so light that sailing ships have been known to be stranded in these "**doldrums**" for weeks at a time. Frequently squalls develop, which can grow into severe hurricanes.

In the tropical waters of the Gulf of Mexico and the Caribbean, these squalls usually form during the months of May and June. From July to October, they form in the Atlantic. Often they begin off Africa's west coast. The squalls build power, whirling winds and great height as they drift west.

On average about 100 storms a year are spotted that could possibly develop hurricane strength. About 10 be-

Paths and directions of some famous hurricanes.

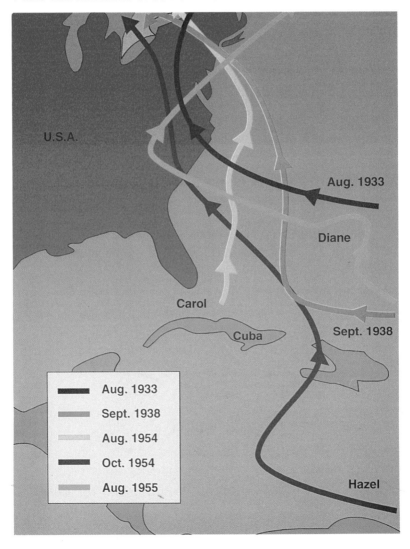

come tropical storms. Of these 6 usually grow into full-scale hurricanes. About 2 strike the United States every year.

Hurricanes usually travel at first in a northwest direction. After hitting land, they tend to turn northeast. They often sweep in a great arc that begins close to the equator. They die as far north as Canada. A big hurricane can cover thousands of miles of land and sea. It can tower ten miles high.

The average hurricane lasts about nine days. The fiercest blasts occur during the storm's first 12 hours onshore.

Hurricane Power

The National Oceanic and Atmospheric Administration (NOAA) controls all U.S. weather research and activities. It divides hurricanes into five categories for its warning system. Category 1 describes small hurricanes with winds of 74 to 95 miles per hour. These carry waves of 4 to 5 feet. Category 5 hurricanes pack winds of over 155 miles per hour. These carry waves higher than 18 feet and cause catastrophic damage.

The average hurricane is as powerful as half a million atomic bombs. Its force, however, is spread out over 300 to 400 miles. Hurricane power has also been estimated to equal 80 earthquakes like the one that destroyed San Francisco in 1906.

A hurricane with winds of 150 miles per hour can hurl 11 tons of pressure against anything it hits. If a house is not sturdily built, it can be smashed or lifted off its foundation. Its roof can be torn off and carried miles away. Cars can be swept away in flash floods or blown over in fierce gales. A hurricane's ocean surge can reach enormous heights, destroying boats and beach houses.

What Causes a Hurricane?

Hurricanes may develop when the sun's rays heat tropical seas to at least 82 degrees Fahrenheit. The air above the heated ocean grows lighter and rises. Water rises with it as vapor, the way boiling water sends up steam. The heat causes the air to rise faster and faster. This is like hot air rising in a chimney.

It takes about half a day for the heated air to begin circling counterclockwise. These winds gradually grow stronger and stronger. They whirl faster and faster. When their speed reaches 75 miles an hour, the winds become a full-fledged hurricane. The faster the winds blow, the more dangerous the hurricane. Some hurricanes develop wind speeds of 200 miles an hour.

These moist, hot winds spiral upward around a calm column of low-pressure air. This is called the **eye.** Occasionally a hurricane develops more than one eye. But there

How hurricane winds begin to form.

is always one main eye, the largest. It measures an average of 15 miles across. Within it there are no storm clouds. There is little or no wind. The sun may even shine here. But beneath the eye the ocean is whipped into a strange, wild, storm-tossed frenzy.

The rising hot winds spin in an increasingly tight spiral around the eye. They rise faster and faster. Cooler air is sucked in behind them. It, too, is heated and sent spiraling up the eye. When the moist, hot air rises high enough, it cools. Then its water vapor forms **droplets.** These cluster together as clouds. The clouds begin to drop rain. The rain is whirled before the hurricane by roaring winds.

We're accustomed to thinking of clouds as weightless, but they are not. A single summer cloud a mile across carries an enormous cargo of seawater. The water would fall with the weight of 70,000 tons if dropped all at once! Imagine the power of a hundred such storm clouds moving together with 200-mile-an-hour roaring winds. Luckily only a few storms at sea become such mighty hurricanes.

A hurricane was once thought to be doughnut shaped. Its rain clouds were believed to circle around a column of calm air. But satellite photos have revealed that the storm is actually shaped more like a pinwheel. Spiraling clouds are thickest close to the eye. Their ends trail off in long, thin streamers.

Basically a hurricane is a huge, churning spiral of powerful, wet winds. These roar around a central pipe of calm air heated by a tropical sea.

The **atmospheric pressure** in a hurricane is always lowest closest to the eye. This makes the winds whirl faster there, from 75 to 200 miles an hour. At the hurricane's outer edges, they blow more slowly, up to 50 miles an hour.

How a Hurricane Builds and Travels

A hurricane's own energy moves it forward. It travels west or northwest at an average speed of ten miles an hour. The heated air rising up the eye swells the clouds. They lift as high as ten miles. Lightning streaks back and forth in the clouds. The winds speed faster and faster around the eye. They also swirl wider and wider, as far as 50 to 100 miles.

As the hurricane travels, it agitates the sea beneath the eye. Ocean water is sucked up like soda in a straw. Ships have reported hurricanes that churned waves as high as a four-story house. This raised water is carried along by the hurricane as a massive hump in the sea.

A hurricane passes over an area in three stages. First, curtains of rain rage in winds traveling as fast as 200 miles an hour. Then the eye arrives. The winds die to a mild

What Hurricane Hugo did to the Sullivan's Island bridge in South Carolina.

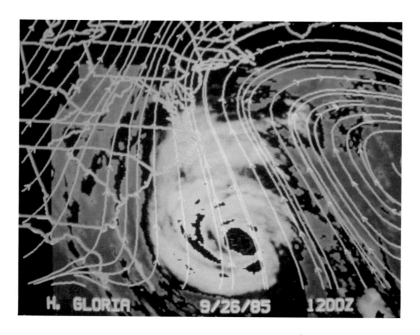

Hurricanes move along with the atmospheric winds. These flow like a river in the atmosphere. But there is no riverbank to contain them. So where they will flow tomorrow is uncertain.

breeze. The rain stops. A sunny blue sky may appear. Just when the storm seems to be over, the third stage of the hurricane strikes. This is the other side of the eye. Once more the full fury of the hurricane travels through.

A hurricane may not advance steadily. It may pause like a great spinning top for perhaps half a day. Then it may suddenly change direction for no apparent reason. Whether it strikes land is just a matter of sheer luck. It may appear to head for shore and then simply blow itself out at sea.

When a hurricane does hit a coast, land friction causes its winds to spiral faster and faster. But after they spend their first fury, the winds gradually weaken. As a hurricane travels north over land, it loses the vapor "fuel" it held from the warm tropical waters. Gradually it slows down.

But until it dies, a hurricane remains powerful enough to inflict dreadful damage. Even after the winds lose their whirling speed, heavy downpours may continue. These can cause severe floods.

HOW THE HURRICANE WARNING SYSTEM DEVELOPED

The earliest hurricane warning system was set up in 1870 as part of the Army Signal Service. Five years later **meteorologist**-priest Father Benito Viñes opened a weather bureau in Havana, Cuba. He collected eyewitness reports from a chain of weather observers around the West Indies. For 18 years, until his death, he telegraphed warnings of approaching hurricanes.

In 1896 a hurricane raged from Florida to Pennsylvania. It killed 114 people, causing $7 million in damage. A public outcry compelled Congress to establish a U.S. Hurricane Warning Service. Weather Bureau chief Willis Moore set up the service's headquarters in Havana. Outlying weather stations reported to it.

Moore appointed Isaac M. Cline chief weather forecaster in Galveston, Texas. In 1900 thousands of Texans gathered to watch huge storm waves give a spectacular show off-shore. Cline dashed through the beach area in a horse and buggy. "Hurricane coming!" he yelled, like a modern Paul Revere. "Leave immediately for higher ground!" Many fled. Others ignored him.

The sky turned black. A wild gale began ripping off slate-roof shingles. They hurtled through the air, killing people they struck. Frightened Texans rushed to escape. They were blown over and rolled along the ground like tumbleweeds.

Storm waves almost two stories high suddenly broke over the city. Galveston was submerged in a 20-foot flood. Houses were torn off their foundations. Ships ripped from anchorage were swept through the streets. Cline's own house collapsed. His wife drowned in the swirling floodwaters.

Some 6,000 Texans lost their lives. Dead bodies of people and animals floated everywhere. Cline called the devastation caused by the hurricane "one of the most horrible sights that ever a civilized people looked upon."

One year later Galveston began building a 17-foot-high seawall. It was so thick it prevented a later hurricane from destroying the city again. Also, Texans no longer ignored hurricane warnings.

(OPPOSITE PAGE) Galveston, Texas, before a severe hurricane struck, September 1900, and (ABOVE) after that hurricane. (BELOW) Bodies being removed from the city after the storm, which killed 6,000 people.

THE HURRICANE HUNTERS

In the 20th century, researchers began to seek ways to monitor and understand hurricanes. In 1935 a radiometeorograph was developed at Harvard University. This instrument measured air pressure, temperature and humidity. A small balloon carried it as high as 95,000 feet where it took its measurements and radioed them back to earth.

In 1943 a new technique was developed that could judge a hurricane's traveling speed, the speed of its interior whirling winds, and how wide an area it covered. That year Major Joseph B. Duckworth, an Army Air Corps flying instructor in Texas, decided to see if a plane could fly through a hurricane on instruments. He and base navigator Ralph O'Hair flew a training plane into a hurricane approaching Galveston.

Their little plane was jolted, tossed, bumped and yanked up and down. They managed to fly through to the calm eye. Then they sought to escape out of the black, swirling gales on the back side of the eye. The hurricane flipped their plane over on its nose. The craft spun around. Duckworth worked the controls furiously. He managed to swing the plane upright. The two flew out of the killer storm and returned to base.

Duckworth's daring flight led to the building of special weather planes to penetrate hurricanes. They became known as Hurricane Hunters. These air force planes patrol both the Atlantic and Pacific oceans. They search for potential hurricanes and typhoons to explore. They stay in the air for as long as 14 hours, flying into, under, over and through potential killer storms.

An air force observer launching balloons to measure wind speeds.

The Hurricane Hunters determine the location, size, wind speeds, air pressure, cloud water content, direction and traveling speeds of hurricanes. This vital information is radioed back to weather stations and the National Hurricane Center in Coral Gables, Florida.

Hurricanes are also probed by "flying laboratories" from NOAA's Aircraft Operations Center in Miami. These planes drop balloons equipped with radio transmitters into the storms. The radios send back continual information to weather stations. Radar can also pick up the information.

A meteorologist tracks the path of a hurricane at the Air Force Global Weather Office, Offutt Air Force Base, Nebraska.

How We're Warned about Hurricanes

The National Hurricane Center gets reports of potential hurricanes by the earliest warning system yet developed— weather satellites. In orbit since 1960, weather satellites send back pictures of cloud covers around the earth. These photos go to the Satellite Center, part of ESSA, the Environmental Science Services Administration. The photos show dark clouds moving in far-reaching spirals. These spirals spotlight developing hurricanes and their locations.

It was a weather satellite that first discovered Hurricane Carla in 1961. The satellite provided warnings early enough to give Texans time to flee the coast.

Additional warning is provided by the National Meteorological Center. Reports from navy and air force weather planes and ships are entered into computers at the center and are studied. There is also SKYWARN, a network of private individuals who observe the weather. As soon as the people spot a destructive storm, they report it to the National Weather Service.

Hurricane tracking is helped by Defense Meteorological Satellites circling the earth.

View from a Hurricane Hunter plane

flying inside the eye of a hurricane.

Air Force Hurricane Hunters flying out to penetrate a probable hurricane.

When whirling cloud formations get close enough, a Hurricane Hunter plane is sent up to explore them. This inspection may verify that the clouds are indeed forming a hurricane that threatens coastal lands. The National Hurricane Center then assigns the storm a name. Radio and TV stations are notified at once. Hurricane Hunters continually fly into the approaching storm to monitor it. Every six hours the center issues "Hurricane Hotline" recorded messages. These describe the hurricane's location, speed, direction and tidal effects.

ESSA's Coast and Geodetic Survey stations watch coastal tides. Higher seas suggest how powerful the water force may be if the hurricane comes ashore. When the hurricane approaches within 200 miles of a coastal area, it is monitored by radar.

Meteorologists at the National Hurricane Center analyze all data received. This helps them estimate when and where the hurricane is likely to strike, how strong it may be, and how long it may last.

As long as the storm remains at sea, the center issues a **hurricane watch** for areas possibly in danger. Once the hurricane heads for land, however, this alert changes to a hurricane warning. A warning means the hurricane may hit within 24 hours. All those in the targeted area are advised to make immediate preparations to flee to higher ground or to storm-proof their homes.

At the National Hurricane Center, Director Robert C. Sheets is interviewed by a Cable News Network reporter (LEFT).

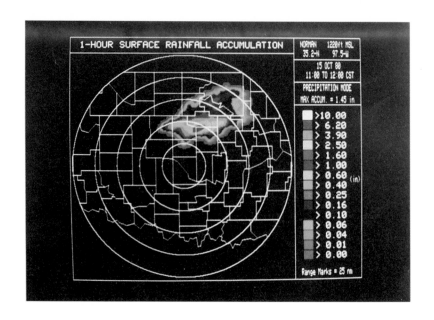

What a weather forecaster sees on his "Next Generation" radar (NEXRAD).

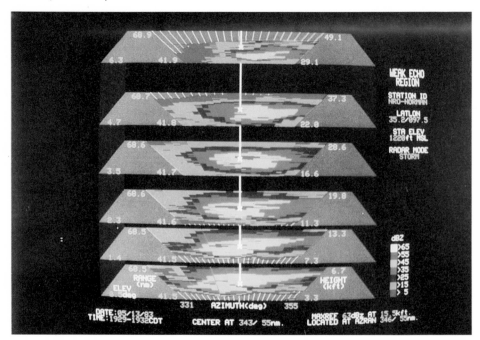

A GOES satellite relaying weather information. Initials stand for Geostationary Operational Environmental Satellite.

The average hurricane warning gives people about 12 to 16 hours advance notice. Sometimes only a 6-hour warning is possible.

When there is danger that a hurricane may cause serious flooding, the center issues a flash flood watch. If the flooding seems very likely, this alert changes to a flash flood warning. Not until a hurricane has lost its power does the center end all its emergency warnings.

The National Hurricane Center has been right 85 percent of the time in forecasts given 18 hours in advance. Moreover, a typical 24-hour forecast made today is actually twice as reliable as one made in the 1960s.

The death toll from hurricanes in the United States has dropped steadily. That's because the center's hurricane tracking and warning system has improved. In the days before the Hurricane Hunters, a 1935 Florida Keys hurricane killed over 400 people. Twenty-five years later the population of the Keys had increased 900 percent. But when Hurricane Donna hit exactly the same area in 1960, the National Hurricane Center's timely warnings emptied the islands. Only three people died.

We are learning more and more about hurricanes through the National Hurricane Research Project. This began in 1955 with the cooperation of the Weather Bureau and several universities.

The Environmental Science Services Administration (ESSA) was organized in 1964. The Weather Bureau was placed under it, along with other scientific agencies. All these collaborate with one another and with international agencies. Together they provide the best possible warnings against hurricanes.

Signs of Hurricane Weather

A hurricane usually sends warning signals of its own. The first sign of its approach is often long, flimsy clouds curving up from the horizon. These are known as **rooster tails.** They indicate where the hurricane is coming from. These clouds gradually grow more numerous until they veil the sky. Then black clouds begin racing overhead.

The full hurricane can be seen rising above the horizon. From a dirty white it turns gray, then black. Winds rise to gale force. They fill the air with salt spray. Ocean waves curl higher and higher, crashing with great power. The whole sky turns black. Lightning flashes streak out. Then . . . the hurricane.

Hurricane clouds photographed by Hurricane Hunter planes.

Lightning streaks from hurricane clouds.

TRYING TO TAME THE HURRICANE

In October 1947 weather planes dropped dry ice into the clouds of a developing hurricane. This was an experiment to try to weaken it at sea. Scientists hoped to force it to release much of its rain power before reaching land. The scheme didn't work. Worse, the hurricane turned abruptly and struck Savannah, Georgia. Angry Georgians did not appreciate the effort.

No further attempts were made until 1958. This time a hurricane at sea was seeded with silver iodine crystals. The results were inconclusive. Some experiments continue to be made. Weather planes fly into hurricanes at altitudes of up to 40,000 feet. They seed hurricanes at different points for two days or longer to try to reduce their power. But so far the effects have been found to be only temporary. Seeded hurricanes regain full force as they continue traveling toward land.

PROTECTING YOURSELF
AGAINST HURRICANES

One should never underestimate the great power of this mighty force of nature. Our best protection lies in heeding NOAA warnings. We need to flee from, or protect ourselves against, an approaching hurricane as rapidly as possible.

Even the thick concrete walls of a house are no certain protection. Hurricane winds can force water into masonry. Saturated walls can weaken and crumble.

Never stay outside to watch a hurricane. Its raging winds are dangerous. Flying objects can strike people. Downed power lines can electrocute the unwary. Huge waves surging ashore can cause devastating floods.

City dwellers should avoid downtown areas. Jagged pieces of blown-out windows from tall buildings can become deadly missiles.

It is also risky to remain in a mobile home or beach house during a hurricane. These can be flattened or blown over. They can also be swept away by flash floods.

When hurricane warnings are issued, people in low-lying areas need to seek shelter. They should go to high ground 15 or 20 miles away from the coast. Hurricanes can bring storm tides of ten feet or higher.

An apartment house (ABOVE) before Hurricane Camille struck in 1969, and (BELOW) the same site after the storm.

Families need to make important preparations as soon as a hurricane watch is issued. They should plan a quick, dependable route out of the area to safer high ground. The family car should be fully gassed and ready. Those who wait until the last minute may find themselves trapped in perilous traffic jams.

Staying home should be considered only when a house is sturdily built on high ground. If you do stay, windows should be protected by securely fastened shutters or boards. They are less apt to shatter if crisscrossed with tape. Gas and water heaters should be readied for shut-off. A stock of canned goods should be kept on hand. A camping stove can provide hot meals if electricity and gas services are lost. Waterproof matches, a lantern, batteries for a radio and flashlight, and a first-aid kit should also be handy. Families living in mobile homes should tie them down firmly with cables.

Fill bathtubs, sinks and big bottles with a supply of water to drink and to flush toilets. Turn the refrigerator to maximum cold. Open it as little as possible. Take everything loose in the yard inside. Leave one or two windows on the side away from the wind slightly open. This will prevent air pressure from building up and blowing out walls. Take pets inside.

Keep the radio tuned to local emergency broadcasts. When the weather alert becomes a hurricane warning, follow the advice of local officials.

During the storm, don't eat possibly spoiled food. Use the most perishable food first. Don't drink tap water or wash food with it until you're sure it isn't contaminated. Avoid using the phone unless absolutely necessary. Phone lines need to be cleared for emergency calls.

When the radio tells you that the storm is finally over, be careful when you venture outside. Avoid downed power lines or the water in which they lie. Steer clear of weakened tree limbs. In snake country watch out for reptiles driven from their homes by flooding.

Beware the Eye!

The arrival of the eye of the hurricane brings deceptively calm weather. Don't be deceived into imagining that the worst is over. Stay inside. The second half of the hurricane will strike shortly, just as fiercely.

People most endangered by hurricanes are sightseers who come out in the eye to view the damage. Or they may watch, swim or ride the high waves. During Hurricane Beulah in 1967, a 15-year-old Texan girl sought thrills surfboarding in the huge waves during the eye. She was drowned when the second half of the hurricane suddenly struck.

HURRICANES TOMORROW

We've learned much about hurricanes in the last 50 years. But scientists still don't really understand why the same conditions sometimes produce hurricanes and sometimes do not.

Nor can weather forecasters predict with certainty the areas a hurricane will hit. Hurricanes often move erratically. They may stop abruptly at sea for hours or days. Or they may circle. Or they may suddenly dart ahead for no apparent reason.

A new study by hurricane expert William M. Gray of Colorado State University revealed dangerous new weather

A Louisiana mansion (ABOVE) from Civil War days before Hurricane Camille struck in 1969, and (BELOW) "gone with the wind."

patterns in the tropical Atlantic off Africa. In a September 1990 issue of *Science* magazine he warned that these patterns may result in more severe hurricanes hitting the East Coast during the next 20 years or so.

Scientists at NOAA continue to analyze hurricane data. Their increased knowledge will provide us with more accurate, earlier warnings.

The need for warnings is becoming increasingly urgent. Millions of Americans are moving into coastal regions in the East and Southeast. Most have had no experience in surviving hurricanes.

NOAA seeks to spur these communities into making hurricane preparations. Public education is vital. Fewer lives will be lost and less damage inflicted as people learn more about these killer storms and how to deal with them.

Some Famous

1737   Bay of Bengal, India: Over 300,000 drowned. Some
       20,000 ships smashed. Four large islands were buried
       under tons of water.

1856   Louisiana coast: A tidal surge smashed every building on
       Last Island. Almost everyone on the island was drowned
       or killed by collapsing hotels.

1881   Haiphong, Vietnam: The port city was flooded and
       destroyed by tidal waves. Death toll: 300,000.

1882   Japanese coast: Japanese navy ships reported a typhoon
       raising frightening waves nine stories high.

1926   Miami: A nine-foot ocean surge swamped docks, streets
       and buildings. The hurricane left 114 dead, destroyed
       25,000 homes, and caused $500 million worth
       of damage.

1928   Florida: A hurricane lifted one end of Lake Okeechobee
       and sent a 25-foot flood crashing over the land.
       Drowned: 25,000. Many were fatally bitten by poisonous
       water moccasins swept up in the flood.

Hurricanes

1938   New York and New England: Storm waves four stories high swamped Long Island. The hurricane took 700 lives, injured 1,500. Over 100,000 homes were damaged or demolished.

1942   Bengal coast, India: A typhoon killed 40,000 people.

1954   Hurricane Carol smashed piers, jetties and cottages from Virginia to New England with 160-mile-an-hour winds. Damage exceeded half a billion dollars.

1954   Hurricane Hazel destroyed the whole business section of Garden City on Long Island, New York. Dead: over 1,000.

1961   Hurricane Carla tossed debris 11 stories high in Galveston, Texas. Homes, docks and boats were destroyed.

1965   Hurricane Betsy did over $6 billion worth of damage to Florida, Mississippi and Louisiana. Over 35,000 people in New Orleans had to be rescued from storm floods by boats and helicopters.

1972   Hurricane Agnes brought massive floods to the whole eastern U.S. seaboard. Drowned: 118. Damage: $2 billion.

Glossary

atmospheric pressure Local atmospheric conditions that send the barometer up or down. Up foretells good weather; down, bad weather.

doldrums Periods of calm winds and light breezes in the tropics.

droplets Tiny drops of sea moisture in clouds.

eye The calm center of a hurricane around which the storm winds whirl.

hurricane An extremely violent, whirling storm that forms over the oceans in the tropics. In the Atlantic, the storm is called a hurricane. In the Pacific, it is known as a **typhoon.**

hurricane warning The next stage of a weather alert after a hurricane watch. It means the storm may hit within 24 hours.

hurricane watch The first weather alert advising people that a hurricane is in the general area.

meteorologist A scientist who studies weather or works in weather forecasting.

rooster tails Long, flimsy clouds seen as a hurricane first approaches an area. They indicate where the hurricane is coming from.

storm Violent disturbance of the atmosphere accompanied by thunder, lightning, rain, snow or hail.

tropics The very warm, humid region lying north and south of the equator. The sun's rays are strongest there.

typhoon A hurricane that arises over the Pacific in the tropics.

For Further Reading

Alth, Max, and Charlotte Alth. *Disastrous Hurricanes and Tornadoes.* New York: Franklin Watts, 1981.

Bixby, William. *Skywatchers.* New York: David McKay Co. 1962.

———. *Hurricanes.* New York: David McKay Co. 1979.

Brindze, Ruth. *Hurricanes: Monster Storms from the Sea.* New York: Atheneum, 1973.

Helm, Thomas. *Hurricane: Weather at Its Worst.* New York: Dodd, Mead & Co., 1967.

Jennings, Gary. *The Killer Storms.* Philadelphia: J. B. Lippincott Co., 1970.

National Oceanic and Atmospheric Administration. *Hurricane: The Greatest Storm on Earth.* Washington, D.C.: U.S. Department of Commerce, n.d.

Winchester, James H. *Hurricanes, Storms, Tornadoes.* New York: G. P. Putnam's Sons, 1968.

INDEX